SELF CARE FOR PEOPLE WITH ADHD

ADHD Self-care Strategies

By

VALATI CLIFFORD

TABLE OF CONTENTS

INTRODUCTION

In a world that often celebrates uniformity and sameness, the journey of an individual with Attention-Deficit/Hyperactivity Disorder (ADHD) can feel like traversing uncharted terrain. If you're holding this book, you've embarked on a unique expedition – one that leads not only to self-discovery but also to the discovery of a treasure trove of potential within you.

ADHD is not a mere label; it's a kaleidoscope of traits that shape the way you experience the world. The twists and turns, the bursts of hyperfocus and the dance of distraction, all come together to paint a canvas that is distinctly yours. But amidst this vibrant canvas, self-care often stands as an overlooked masterpiece, waiting to be nurtured.

The pages that follow are an invitation to pause, reflect, and embark on a journey of self-care that is tailored to your unique needs. It's a journey that acknowledges the challenges you face and the brilliance you possess. In this book, we're not just exploring self-care tips; we're exploring self-acceptance, resilience, and growth.

Embracing your ADHD journey means daring to look beyond societal norms and expectations. It means reclaiming your narrative and steering it toward empowerment. This journey isn't about erasing ADHD; it's about embracing it. It's about understanding that the quirks and complexities that come with ADHD are the same ones that make you capable of incredible feats.

Throughout these chapters, you'll find stories – stories of triumphs and trials, stories that echo your experiences, and stories that remind you that you're not alone on this path. You'll find practical strategies rooted in mindfulness, time management, and emotional well-being, but you'll also find the encouragement to find your own path, your own rhythm.

Embracing your ADHD journey isn't a sprint; it's a marathon that requires patience, self-compassion, and an unwavering belief in your potential. The chapters ahead are not just about reading; they're about engaging, reflecting, and taking meaningful steps toward a life that's not defined by limitations but enriched by possibilities.

So, let's embark on this expedition together. Let's challenge conventions and celebrate uniqueness. Let's weave a narrative that's rich in self-care and self-discovery. Are you ready to embrace your ADHD journey? The adventure begins now.

CHAPTER ONE

UNDERSTANDING ADHD

In a world pulsating with information and demands, the term "ADHD" is often tossed around casually, its true complexity often overshadowed by misconceptions and stereotypes. But beneath the surface lies a multidimensional neurological condition that shapes the lives of millions. Understanding ADHD requires us to go beyond the surface, to unravel the layers of intricacy that define this enigmatic condition.

A Spectrum of Attention:

Attention-Deficit/Hyperactivity Disorder, or ADHD, is not a one-size-fits-all diagnosis. It's a spectrum, ranging from the predominantly inattentive type, where focus wanes like a flickering candle, to the predominantly hyperactive-impulsive type, where thoughts and actions are a whirlwind. Then there's the combined type, a symphony of both. Each type brings its own set of challenges and strengths, painting a unique portrait of cognitive diversity.

Neurodiversity at Play:
It's important to view ADHD through the lens of neurodiversity. Just as biodiversity is essential for a thriving ecosystem, neurodiversity enriches the human experience. ADHD brains are wired differently, processing information in ways that can result in breathtaking creativity, lightning-fast problem-solving, and the ability to hyperfocus on tasks of deep interest. Yet, these same brains can grapple with regulating attention, impulsivity, and emotional responses.

Beyond Just Attention:
Contrary to popular belief, ADHD is not merely a challenge of attention. It's a symphony of interconnected traits. Emotional dysregulation can transform minor setbacks into emotional roller coasters. Executive function, the conductor

of cognitive processes, can struggle to manage time, organize thoughts, and plan ahead. Rejection sensitivity can magnify the impact of criticism, even if it's unintended.

The Nature vs. Nurture Conundrum: The origins of ADHD are shrouded in the intricate interplay of genetics and environment. It's a dance of nature vs. nurture, with genetic predisposition interacting with factors such as prenatal exposure to toxins, childhood adversity, and even parenting styles. This complexity has led to an ongoing quest to uncover the biological underpinnings that make ADHD what it is.

Breaking the Stigma: ADHD often battles stigma, misconstrued as mere laziness or lack of discipline. But it's essential to debunk these myths. ADHD individuals might struggle with focus, but their brains also possess the capacity for deep concentration when aligned with their passions. The journey isn't about erasing ADHD but about harnessing its strengths and managing its challenges.

Towards Empathy and Support:
Understanding ADHD is not a solitary endeavor; it's a collective responsibility. Schools, workplaces, and communities must strive to create environments that accommodate diverse cognitive styles. This starts with education that fosters empathy and cultivates awareness of ADHD's nuances.

The Complex Tapestry:
As we attempt to understand ADHD, we're unraveling a complex tapestry woven with threads of brilliance, challenge, and resilience. It's a journey that requires a commitment to dispelling misconceptions and embracing the rich diversity that ADHD brings to the human experience.

In the end, understanding ADHD is an ongoing exploration, an ever-evolving journey of comprehension, compassion, and collaboration. It's about recognizing that within complexity lies a world of potential waiting to be unlocked, one that enriches not only the lives of those with ADHD but the entire fabric of society.

THE ESSENCE OF SELF-CARE:
In the midst of our bustling lives, the term "self-care" has become a ubiquitous buzzword, often accompanied by images of spa days, scented candles, and bubble baths. While these moments of indulgence certainly have their place, the true essence of self-care extends far beyond the surface-level trends and commodified ideals that dominate social media. It's a concept that invites us to embark on a profound journey of self-discovery, growth, and holistic well-being.

At its core, self-care is a commitment to prioritize and nurture our physical, mental, emotional, and spiritual health. It's not merely about momentary escapes from reality but rather about creating a sustainable foundation that allows us to navigate life's challenges with resilience and authenticity. While the world entices us with instant gratification, genuine self-care encourages us to look inward and ask ourselves some essential questions: Who am I? What do I truly need? How can I cultivate a life that aligns with my values?

In a society that glorifies busyness and achievement, practicing self-care can often be misconstrued as selfish or indulgent. However, this perspective fails to recognize that nurturing ourselves is a fundamental prerequisite for effectively engaging with the world around us. Just as a well-tended garden blooms vibrantly, our lives flourish when we take the time to nurture our own well-being. This doesn't mean neglecting responsibilities or shutting ourselves off from the world; rather, it empowers us to show up as our best selves in all aspects of life.

True self-care is multi-faceted, encompassing various dimensions of our existence. At the physical level, it involves nourishing our bodies with wholesome food, regular exercise, and sufficient rest. It's recognizing that our bodies are not mere vessels but intricate ecosystems that require care and attention. Likewise, mental self-care encourages us to cultivate a positive relationship with our thoughts and embrace mindfulness practices that quiet the relentless chatter of our minds.

Emotional self-care delves into the realm of our feelings, urging us to acknowledge and process our emotions rather than suppressing or denying them. This involves seeking support when needed, setting healthy boundaries, and engaging in activities that bring us joy and fulfillment. Moreover, spiritual self-care invites us to explore our beliefs, connect with a sense of purpose, and foster a deeper understanding of ourselves and the world.

The journey of self-care is not always comfortable. It's not just about pampering ourselves; it's about doing the inner work required for growth and transformation. This means confronting our insecurities, facing our fears, and addressing the aspects of ourselves we may have neglected. It's about recognizing that genuine self-care isn't always glamorous; it's about doing the hard work to heal, evolve, and become more resilient.

Self-care is not a one-size-fits-all prescription. It's a deeply personal journey that requires us to listen to our own needs and preferences. What brings restoration to one person's soul might not resonate with another. It's about experimenting with various practices and finding what genuinely rejuvenates us. From solitary hikes in nature to engaging in creative pursuits, from practicing meditation to spending quality time with loved ones, self-care takes on myriad forms.

Furthermore, self-care isn't a destination but an ongoing process. It's a commitment to regularly assess our well-being and make adjustments as needed. This might involve reevaluating our priorities, saying no to commitments that drain us, and embracing change when it's necessary for our growth. Just as we wouldn't expect a single workout session to grant us lasting physical fitness, genuine self-care requires consistent effort and dedication.

In a world that bombards us with distractions and external demands, practicing self-care can be challenging. It requires us to reclaim our time and energy, resisting the pull of constant busyness and cultivating a deeper connection with ourselves. It might mean disconnecting from technology, creating space for solitude, and allowing ourselves to simply be without the need for productivity.

Ultimately, the essence of self-care extends beyond the surface-level clichés and fleeting indulgences. It's a profound act of self-love and empowerment that ripples outward, influencing how we engage with our communities and contribute to the world. When we prioritize our well-being, we become better equipped to show up for others and create positive change. It's a reminder that self-care is not selfish; it's a necessary foundation for a life that is purposeful, authentic, and aligned with our true selves.

In conclusion, self-care transcends the realm of trends and buzzwords. It's a transformative journey that calls us to explore the depths of our being, prioritize our well-being, and embrace growth with open arms. Beyond the face masks and scented candles lies a profound invitation to cultivate a life that is balanced, meaningful, and in harmony with our authentic selves. So, let us embark on this journey of self-discovery and self-nurturing, for in doing so, we unlock the potential to live a life that truly resonates with our heart's deepest desires.

Building Your ADHD Self-Care Foundation

Living with Attention Deficit Hyperactivity Disorder (ADHD) presents unique challenges, but establishing a strong foundation of self-care can greatly improve your quality of life. By adopting tailored strategies and embracing self-awareness, you can effectively manage ADHD symptoms and enhance your overall well-being.

Prioritize Routine and Structure:
Establishing a consistent daily routine can help you manage time and tasks more effectively. Set regular sleep patterns, allocate specific times for work and breaks, and create to-do lists to maintain focus and productivity.

Building a strong foundation of self-care is essential for effectively managing ADHD. By embracing routines, practicing mindfulness, staying organized, and seeking support, you can navigate the challenges posed by ADHD and lead a fulfilling and balanced life. Remember, every individual's journey is unique, so it's important to find the strategies that work best for you.

CHAPTER TWO

ACKNOWLEDGING YOUR UNIQUE NEEDS

Acknowledging your unique needs is an essential aspect of effective communication and relationship building. It involves recognizing that each individual has distinct requirements, preferences, and circumstances that influence how they perceive and interact with the world. Here's a detailed perspective on this concept:

Individuality and Diversity: Every person is unique due to their background, experiences, beliefs, values, and personality traits. Acknowledging these differences demonstrates respect for their identity and helps create an inclusive environment.

Empathy and Understanding: To acknowledge someone's unique needs, it's important to cultivate empathy and actively seek to understand their perspective. This involves listening attentively, asking questions, and putting yourself in their shoes to grasp their thoughts and emotions.

Open Communication: Encouraging open and honest communication is crucial. This allows individuals to express their needs, preferences, and concerns freely, fostering an atmosphere of trust and collaboration.

Personalized Approach: Tailoring your interactions and solutions to suit the individual's requirements showcases that you value their distinctiveness. This could apply to customer service, education, healthcare, and any context where you're dealing with people.

Flexibility: Being flexible in your approach shows that you are adaptable to the evolving needs of individuals. This might mean adjusting your plans, strategies, or even your thinking to accommodate their specific circumstances.

Respectful Feedback: When seeking feedback or providing it, acknowledge that different perspectives exist. This shows that you're open to learning from others and willing to make improvements based on their input.

Inclusion and Accessibility: Consider accessibility in all aspects of your interactions, whether it's designing physical spaces, websites, or content. Making accommodations for people with disabilities is a tangible way of acknowledging diverse needs.

Customization: In business, offering customizable products or services lets customers choose what best suits their requirements. This acknowledges that a one-size-fits-all approach isn't always effective.

Cultural Sensitivity: Be aware of cultural differences that can influence how individuals communicate and interpret messages. Respect and honor these cultural nuances to avoid misunderstandings.

Long-term Relationships: Acknowledging unique needs is a foundation for building strong, lasting relationships. It fosters loyalty and mutual understanding, making interactions more meaningful.

Problem Solving: When faced with challenges, approach problem-solving by taking into account the various needs of those involved. This leads to solutions that are more comprehensive and effective.

Personal Growth: Acknowledging the unique needs of others also promotes personal growth and development. It encourages you to expand your perspectives and learn from others' experiences.

In summary, acknowledging unique needs involves a combination of empathy, open communication, customization, and cultural sensitivity. It's a fundamental aspect of respectful and effective interactions that can enhance relationships, problem-solving, and personal growth.

Embracing Your Strengths

Embracing your strengths is a powerful way to unlock your full potential. Recognize your unique abilities and talents, and focus on nurturing them. When you acknowledge your strengths, you can set goals that align with them, boost your confidence, and find greater satisfaction in your pursuits. Remember, everyone has their own set of strengths – it's about harnessing them to create a positive impact in your life and the lives of others.

Be open to feedback and reflect on what comes naturally to you. Leverage these qualities in various aspects of your life, whether it's in your career, relationships, or personal hobbies. Don't be afraid to showcase your strengths and use them to your advantage, as they can set you apart and make you more resilient in the face of challenges.

It's important to note that embracing your strengths doesn't mean ignoring your weaknesses. Acknowledge areas where you may not excel and consider how your strengths can complement those areas. Sometimes, collaborating with others who have strengths in your weaker areas can lead to more well-rounded outcomes.

Remember, growth is a continuous process. Regularly assess and refine your strengths as you evolve. Embracing your strengths allows you to build a foundation for a more authentic, fulfilling life where you can truly shine.

Setting Realistic Expectations

Setting realistic expectations is crucial for personal well-being and success. It involves understanding your capabilities, resources, and the constraints of a situation. By setting achievable goals, you can avoid unnecessary stress and disappointment. It's important to consider your current circumstances, time constraints, and available resources when determining what you can realistically accomplish. This doesn't mean aiming low, but rather setting goals that challenge you while still being attainable. Remember, achieving smaller, realistic goals can lead to a more sustainable path toward your larger aspirations.

Assess Your Situation: Take a clear and objective look at your current situation. Consider your strengths, limitations, and the external factors that might impact your goals.goals

Prioritize: Not all goals are equally important. Focus on what matters most and allocate your time and resources accordingly.

Learn from Past Experiences: Reflect on previous instances where your expectations might have been unrealistic. What can you learn from those situations to make better judgments now?

Seek Input: Discuss your goals and expectations with others who have relevant experience or knowledge. Their insights can provide valuable perspectives and help you refine your expectations.

Flexibility: Life is unpredictable. Be prepared to adapt your expectations if circumstances change, without feeling discouraged.

Celebrate Progress: Acknowledge and celebrate the milestones you achieve along the way. This helps to maintain motivation and a positive mindset.

Incorporating these principles into your approach can lead to a more balanced and fulfilling pursuit of your goals.

Mindfulness and ADHD: Cultivating Present Moment Awareness

Mindfulness, the practice of being fully present in the moment, is gaining attention as a valuable tool for individuals with Attention Deficit Hyperactivity Disorder (ADHD). In a world that often feels fast-paced and demanding, mindfulness offers a way to anchor oneself, manage symptoms, and enhance overall well-being.

For individuals with ADHD, staying focused and managing impulses can be challenging.

Mindfulness provides a path to develop greater self-awareness and self-regulation. By training the mind to pay attention intentionally and without judgment, individuals can cultivate a better understanding of their thoughts, emotions, and behaviors.

The practice of mindfulness involves simple techniques like deep breathing, body scans, and meditation. These techniques help create a space between stimuli and reactions, allowing individuals to respond more thoughtfully rather than impulsively. Mindfulness doesn't eliminate ADHD symptoms, but it equips individuals with tools to navigate them more effectively.

Research suggests that regular mindfulness practice can lead to improved attention, reduced impulsivity, and better emotional regulation for those with ADHD. It also contributes to lower levels of stress and anxiety, common companions of ADHD. By embracing the present moment, individuals can break the cycle of rumination about the past or worry about the future that often accompanies ADHD.

Incorporating mindfulness into daily life requires patience and consistency. Start with short sessions and gradually increase the duration. Mindful practices can be integrated into routines, such as mindful eating or taking mindful breaks during the day. Mobile apps, online resources, and guided sessions can offer structured support.

It's important to note that mindfulness is not a replacement for other ADHD management strategies. It's most effective when used in combination with medication, therapy, and lifestyle adjustments. Consulting a healthcare professional before starting any new practice is advised.

In a world filled with distractions, mindfulness empowers individuals with ADHD to embrace the present moment, enhance self-awareness, and cultivate a greater sense of calm amidst the chaos. Through practice and patience, it becomes a valuable tool in the journey towards managing ADHD symptoms and living a more fulfilling life.

Harnessing Impulsivity through Mindfulness

Impulsivity, a common challenge for many, can lead to hasty decisions and regrets. Mindfulness offers a valuable approach to understanding and managing impulsive behaviors, allowing individuals to pause and make more intentional choices.

Mindfulness involves paying deliberate attention to the present moment, observing thoughts and emotions without judgment. For those struggling with impulsivity, this practice creates a mental gap between the impulse and the action. Here's how mindfulness can help harness impulsivity:

Increased Awareness: Mindfulness cultivates self-awareness, helping individuals recognize impulsive urges as they arise. By acknowledging these urges without immediate action, individuals can choose a more thoughtful response.

Creating Space: Mindfulness provides a mental space to evaluate options before acting. It allows individuals to consider the potential consequences of their actions and make decisions aligned with their values.

Emotion Regulation: Impulsivity often stems from intense emotions. Mindfulness encourages acknowledging emotions without reacting impulsively. Over time, individuals learn to manage emotional reactions and respond in a balanced way.

Observing Urges: Mindfulness trains individuals to observe impulses without judgment. This empowers them to detach from the urgency of the moment and make decisions driven by reason rather than fleeting desires.

Mindful Breathing: Deep breathing techniques are integral to mindfulness. When faced with an impulsive urge, taking a few deep breaths can provide the space needed to pause and make a conscious choice.

Mindful Action: Mindfulness doesn't mean eliminating spontaneity. It's about consciously choosing when to act on impulses and when to exercise restraint for better outcomes.

Reducing Regret: By cultivating mindfulness, individuals can prevent impulsive actions that often lead to regret.

This contributes to improved self-esteem and a sense of control.

Practicing mindfulness requires dedication and patience. Starting with short sessions and gradually integrating mindful moments into daily life can be highly effective. Over time, mindfulness becomes a tool to manage impulsivity, leading to healthier decisions and improved relationships.

In a world that encourages instant gratification, mindfulness empowers individuals to navigate the complexities of impulsivity with greater awareness and intention. As mindfulness becomes a part of one's routine, the journey toward self-mastery and well-considered choices unfolds, one mindful breath at a time.

CHAPTER THREE

TIME MANAGEMENT AND ORGANIZATION STRATEGIES

In today's fast-paced world, the ability to effectively manage time and stay organized is a crucial skill. Whether you're a student, a professional, or someone juggling multiple responsibilities, employing the right time management and organization strategies can significantly boost your productivity and reduce stress. In this article, we'll explore some proven techniques to help you master these skills and make the most of every day.

1. Prioritize Tasks with the Eisenhower Matrix:

The Eisenhower Matrix, also known as the Urgent-Important Matrix, is a valuable tool for categorizing tasks based on their urgency and importance. Divide your tasks into four quadrants: Urgent and Important,

Important but Not Urgent, Urgent but Not Important, and Neither Urgent nor Important. This method helps you focus on tasks that truly matter while minimizing distractions.

2. Set SMART Goals:
SMART goals are Specific, Measurable, Achievable, Relevant, and Time-Bound. When setting goals, ensure they are well-defined and realistic. This approach provides clarity and motivation, making it easier to track progress and stay on target.

3. Utilize the Pomodoro Technique:
The Pomodoro Technique involves breaking your work into short, focused intervals (typically 25 minutes) followed by a short break. After completing a set of intervals, take a longer break. This method harnesses the power of focused bursts of work, enhancing productivity while preventing burnout.

4. Maintain a To-Do List:

A to-do list is a classic yet effective way to keep track of tasks. Write down your tasks for the day or week, and as you complete each task, cross it off. This not only gives you a sense of accomplishment but also keeps you organized and informed about what needs to be done next.

5. Declutter Your Workspace:

An organized workspace promotes concentration and efficiency. Regularly declutter your physical and digital spaces, keeping only what you need for your immediate tasks. A clean environment can reduce distractions and help you stay focused.

6. Use Digital Tools:

There are numerous digital tools and apps designed to aid time management and organization. Calendar apps like Google Calendar can help you schedule tasks and appointments, while task management apps like Todoist or Trello assist in organizing your tasks and projects.

7. Learn to Say No:
Saying no when necessary is essential for protecting your time and maintaining your priorities. Politely decline tasks or commitments that don't align with your goals or would overwhelm your schedule.

8. Batch Similar Tasks:
Grouping similar tasks together and completing them in one go can save time and mental energy. For instance, respond to emails in specific time blocks rather than sporadically throughout the day.

9. Reflect and Review:
Regularly assess your progress and evaluate your strategies. What's working? What needs adjustment? Reflection allows you to refine your approach and make necessary changes to optimize your time management and organization techniques.

10. Take Care of Yourself:
Remember that effective time management isn't just about work; it's about maintaining a healthy balance. Prioritize self-care, including adequate sleep, exercise, and relaxation. A well-rested and rejuvenated mind is more capable of efficient and organized work.

In conclusion, mastering time management and organization strategies is an ongoing journey that requires commitment and practice. By prioritizing tasks, setting clear goals, and using techniques like the Pomodoro Technique and the Eisenhower Matrix, you can enhance your productivity and reduce stress. Combined with maintaining a clutter-free workspace and utilizing digital tools, these strategies can help you make the most of each day while maintaining a healthy work-life balance. Remember, effective time management isn't about adding more to your plate; it's about optimizing what's already there.

CREATING ADHD-FRIENDLY ROUTINES: Navigating Life with Structure and Flexibility

Living with ADHD (Attention Deficit Hyperactivity Disorder) presents unique challenges in managing time, staying organized, and maintaining focus. However, with the right strategies and a supportive routine, individuals with ADHD can thrive. Building routines that are tailored to the characteristics of ADHD can provide a sense of structure and predictability, while also allowing for the necessary flexibility. In this article, we'll explore some tips for creating ADHD-friendly routines that work.

1. Embrace Visual Cues:
Visual cues are powerful tools for individuals with ADHD. Use color-coded calendars, sticky notes, or digital apps with

visual interfaces to help organize tasks, appointments, and deadlines. These cues make information more accessible and engaging.

2. Break Tasks into Smaller Steps:

Large tasks can feel overwhelming for individuals with ADHD. Break them down into smaller, manageable steps. This approach provides a sense of accomplishment with each completed step, making it easier to stay motivated and focused.

3. Set Time Blocks:

Utilize the Pomodoro Technique by allocating specific time blocks for tasks. Work on a task for a set amount of time, followed by a short break. This structure helps manage attention spans and prevents burnout.

4. Prioritize with the Two-Minute Rule:

If a task can be completed in two minutes or less, do it immediately. This rule prevents small tasks from accumulating and becoming overwhelming.

5. Create Consistent Daily Routines: Consistency is key for individuals with ADHD. Establish a daily routine that includes regular sleep, meal, and exercise times. This consistency can improve overall focus and emotional regulation.

6. Use External Reminders: Leverage external reminders such as alarms, alerts, and notifications to stay on track. Set reminders for important tasks, appointments, and medication schedules.

7. Limit Distractions: Designate specific areas for focused work or study. Minimize distractions by keeping these areas clutter-free and free from unnecessary stimuli.

8. Include Physical Movement:
Incorporate physical activity breaks into your routine. Movement can help regulate attention and energy levels. Consider taking short walks or engaging in quick stretches.

9. Flexibility and Self-Compassion:
Recognize that flexibility is a crucial aspect of ADHD-friendly routines. Be compassionate with yourself when unexpected changes occur. Adapt your routine as needed without feeling discouraged.

10. Reflect and Adjust:
Regularly evaluate your routine's effectiveness. What's working well? What needs improvement? Adjustments might be necessary to better suit your needs and changing circumstances.

11. Mindfulness and Meditation:
Practicing mindfulness and meditation can enhance self-awareness and improve focus.

These techniques can also help manage impulsivity and hyperactivity.

12. Seek Professional Guidance:
If building an ADHD-friendly routine feels challenging, consider working with a mental health professional or ADHD coach. They can provide personalized strategies and support tailored to your specific needs.

In conclusion, creating an ADHD-friendly routine involves combining structure and flexibility to accommodate the unique characteristics of ADHD. Visual cues, breaking tasks into smaller steps, and setting time blocks are just a few strategies that can enhance productivity and organization. Remember that finding the right routine might take time and experimentation, and it's okay to seek guidance along the way. With patience, self-awareness, and the right tools, individuals with ADHD can build routines that empower them to succeed in various aspects of life.

Taming the Time Perception Challenge: Navigating the Complexities of Perceived Time

The concept of time is both universal and deeply personal. However, the way we perceive time can be influenced by various factors, leading to challenges in managing our schedules and tasks effectively. This phenomenon, known as time perception, has significant implications for our productivity, well-being, and overall sense of control. In this article, we'll explore the complexities of time perception and provide strategies to help you navigate this challenge.

Understanding Time Perception:
Time perception refers to the subjective experience of time passing. While the clock ticks at a constant rate, our perception of

time can vary greatly based on psychological, emotional, and situational factors. When we're engaged in an enjoyable activity, time often seems to fly by, whereas periods of boredom or stress can make time feel agonizingly slow.

Factors Influencing Time Perception: Several factors contribute to the distortions in time perception:

Novelty and Routine: Engaging in novel experiences can make time appear longer, as our brains process more information. Conversely, routine activities may seem to pass quickly due to their predictability.

Age: Time perception changes as we age. Younger individuals tend to perceive time as passing more slowly than older individuals.

Attention and Engagement: When fully immersed in an activity, time tends to feel faster. Conversely, feeling bored or distracted can make time drag.

Emotional States: Strong emotions, both positive and negative, can alter our perception of time. Anxious moments might feel prolonged, while joyful occasions might seem fleeting.

Cultural and Social Influences: Cultural norms and societal expectations can impact how time is perceived. Different cultures may place varying emphasis on punctuality and planning.

Immerse Yourself: Engage in activities that fully capture your attention and passion. When you're engrossed, time tends to fly by.

Practice Patience: In situations where time feels slow, practicing patience and acceptance can alleviate the frustration that often accompanies perceived slowness.

Stay Organized: Efficiently managing tasks and responsibilities can prevent feelings of time slipping away. Utilize calendars and to-do lists to maintain a sense of control.

Reflect and Reframe: Regularly reflect on your experiences with time. Identify patterns in your perception and consider reframing how you approach activities that tend to make time drag.

In conclusion, taming the time perception challenge requires a combination of self-awareness, mindfulness, and adaptive strategies. By understanding the factors that influence our perception of time and implementing techniques to manage it, we can enhance our productivity, well-being, and overall satisfaction with how we experience the passage of time. Remember that time perception is subjective, and finding the right balance between routine and novelty can help you make the most of each moment.

ORGANIZING YOUR ENVIRONMENT FOR SUCCESS: Creating a Productive and Inspiring Space

The environment in which we live and work plays a significant role in our productivity, creativity, and overall well-being. An organized and well-designed space can greatly enhance our ability to focus, stay motivated, and achieve our goals. In this article, we'll explore effective strategies for organizing your environment to set the stage for success.

1. **Declutter Regularly:**
Clutter can be a major distraction and source of stress. Regularly declutter your space by getting rid of items you no longer need or use. Keep only what is essential and meaningful to create a clean and organized environment.

2. Designate Functional Zones:
Divide your space into functional zones based on your activities. Create separate areas for work, relaxation, exercise, and hobbies. This separation helps signal your brain for specific tasks and prevents mixing work and leisure.

3. Arrange for Ergonomics:
Ensure your furniture and equipment are set up in an ergonomic manner. Your chair, desk, and computer should be positioned to promote good posture and comfort, reducing physical strain during long periods of work.

4. Utilize Storage Solutions:
Invest in storage solutions that fit your space and needs. Shelving, drawers, baskets, and organizers can help keep items organized and easily accessible.

5. Keep a Clear Workspace:

Maintain a clutter-free workspace to enhance focus and efficiency. Only have the essentials on your desk, such as your computer, notebook, and a few necessary supplies.

6. Personalize Your Space:
Add personal touches to your environment, such as photos, artwork, or plants. These elements can make the space more inviting and inspire creativity.

7. Manage Digital Clutter:
Organize your digital environment as well. Create folders, use consistent file naming conventions, and regularly clean up your computer desktop to reduce digital clutter.

8. Use Color and Lighting:
Colors and lighting can influence your mood and energy levels. Choose colors that promote the atmosphere you desire. Additionally, ensure adequate natural and artificial lighting to prevent eye strain.

9. Implement a Filing System:

For physical documents, establish a clear filing system. Label folders and containers appropriately to easily locate important papers when needed.

10. Minimize Distractions:

Identify potential distractions in your environment and take steps to minimize them. This could involve noise-cancelling headphones, closing unnecessary tabs on your computer, or setting boundaries with others.

11. Plan for Accessibility:

Arrange frequently used items within easy reach. This prevents unnecessary movement and disruption of your workflow.

12. Regular Maintenance:

Once you've organized your environment, commit to regular maintenance. Set aside time each week to tidy up, declutter, and reevaluate your organization strategies.

In conclusion, organizing your environment for success is about creating a space that supports your goals, activities, and overall mindset. A well-organized environment can improve your focus, boost creativity, and reduce stress. By incorporating strategies such as decluttering, functional zoning, and maintaining ergonomic setups, you can design a space that empowers you to achieve your aspirations and lead a more balanced and productive life.

CHAPTER FOUR

NURTURING MENTAL AND EMOTIONAL WELL-BEING

Nurturing mental and emotional well-being is crucial for maintaining a balanced and fulfilling life. Here's a detailed guide on how to achieve this:

Healthy diet: A balanced diet rich in nutrients can positively impact brain function and mood. Omega-3 fatty acids, whole grains, fruits, and vegetables are beneficial.

Adequate sleep: Quality sleep is essential for cognitive function and emotional regulation. Maintain a consistent sleep schedule and create a relaxing bedtime routine.routine

Limit screen time: Excessive screen time, especially on social media, can lead to negative comparisons and impact mental well-being. Set boundaries for your digital interactions.

Engage in hobbies: Pursue activities that bring joy and satisfaction. Hobbies provide an outlet for self-expression and can serve as a form of relaxation.

Practice gratitude: Regularly reflect on things you're thankful for. This cultivates a positive outlook and shifts focus away from negativity.

Limit negative self-talk: Challenge negative thoughts and replace them with more balanced and positive ones.

Practice self-compassion: Treat yourself with the same kindness you would offer to a friend. Be forgiving of mistakes and setbacks.

Cultivate resilience: Develop the ability to bounce back from adversity. View challenges as opportunities for growth and learning.

Engage in laughter: Laughter releases endorphins and promotes relaxation. Watch a funny movie, spend time with friends who make you laugh, or find humor in everyday situations.

Remember, nurturing mental and emotional well-being is an ongoing process. It requires commitment, patience, and self-compassion. Regularly assess your well-being and make adjustments to your lifestyle as needed.

MANAGING OVERWHELM AND REJECTION SENSITIVITY

Managing overwhelm and rejection sensitivity can be challenging, but with some strategies, you can navigate these feelings more effectively:

Managing Overwhelm:

Prioritize: Break tasks into smaller, manageable steps. Focus on completing one task at a time rather than looking at the big picture.

Learn to Say No: Don't overcommit. Politely decline tasks or activities that add unnecessary stress to your plate.

Practice Mindfulness: Engage in mindfulness techniques, such as deep breathing or meditation, to bring your focus to the present moment and reduce anxiety about the future.

Set Boundaries: Clearly define your limits with others. This could include setting limits on work hours, social commitments, or digital interactions.

Delegate: If possible, delegate tasks to others to lighten your load and share responsibilities.

Seek Support: Talk to friends, family, or a therapist about your feelings of overwhelm. Sometimes, just discussing your challenges can provide relief.

Focus on Your Strengths: Remind yourself of your strengths and accomplishments. This can help counteract feelings of inadequacy.

Cognitive Behavioral Therapy (CBT): CBT techniques can help rewire negative thought patterns and reactions to rejection.

Remember that managing overwhelm and rejection sensitivity is an ongoing process. It's okay to seek professional help if these feelings significantly impact your daily life or well-being. A therapist can provide personalized strategies and support tailored to your specific situation.

NAVIGATING RELATIONSHIPS WITH ADHD

Navigating relationships when one or both partners have ADHD (Attention-Deficit/Hyperactivity Disorder) can require understanding, communication, and patience. Here are some tips to help:

Educate Yourself: Learn about ADHD, its symptoms, and how it can affect relationships. Understanding the challenges it presents will promote empathy and better communication.

Open Communication: Talk openly with your partner about ADHD. Discuss its impact on both of you and share your feelings, concerns, and needs.

Set Clear Expectations: Establish clear expectations for communication, responsibilities, and time management. Having a shared understanding can prevent misunderstandings.

Structure and Routine: Create routines and structures that help manage time and responsibilities. This can provide stability and predictability, which are often helpful for individuals with ADHD.

Active Listening: Practice active listening when your partner speaks. Show empathy and provide them with your full attention.

Break Tasks Down: Divide tasks into smaller, manageable steps. This can make tasks feel less overwhelming and improve follow-through.

Use Visual Aids: Visual aids like calendars, to-do lists, and reminders can be very helpful in managing daily tasks and appointments.

Limit Distractions: Minimize distractions when having important conversations. Find a quiet and focused environment to engage in meaningful discussions.

Compromise and Flexibility: Understand that both partners may need to compromise and be flexible to accommodate each other's needs and challenges.

Emotional Support: Offer emotional support to your partner. Validate their feelings and reassure them that you're there to help.

Celebrate Small Wins: Celebrate achievements and milestones, even if they are small. Positive reinforcement can motivate both partners.

Quality Time: Dedicate quality time to connect and bond with each other. This can strengthen the emotional connection between partners.

Manage Impulsivity: For the partner with ADHD, work on managing impulsive behaviors and reactions. Practice pausing before responding.

Remember that each relationship is unique, and what works for one couple might not work for another. The key is to communicate openly, show empathy, and work together to find strategies that support both partners' well-being and the health of the relationship.

CHAPTER FIVE

PHYSICAL HEALTH AND ADHD

Physical health can significantly impact ADHD symptoms. Regular exercise, a balanced diet, sufficient sleep, and managing stress can all contribute to better symptom management. Exercise, in particular, has been shown to improve focus and executive function in individuals with ADHD. It's important to consult a healthcare professional to create a tailored plan that combines both physical and behavioral strategies for managing ADHD effectively.

EXERCISE AS A TOOL FOR FOCUS AND CALM

Exercise is one of the powerful tool for enhancing focus and promoting calmness, especially for individuals dealing with conditions like ADHD. Engaging in regular physical activity has been shown to have numerous benefits on cognitive function and mental well-being.

Improved Neurotransmitter Balance: Exercise increases the release of neurotransmitters like dopamine, norepinephrine, and serotonin. These chemicals play a crucial role in regulating mood, attention, and impulse control – areas often affected by ADHD.

Enhanced Executive Function: Executive functions such as planning, organization, and time management can be challenging for individuals with ADHD. Exercise has been linked to improvements in these functions by stimulating the prefrontal cortex, the brain region responsible for executive control.

Increased Blood Flow to the Brain: Physical activity boosts blood flow to the brain, delivering oxygen and nutrients that support cognitive functions. This increased circulation can contribute to better concentration and mental clarity.

Stress Reduction: Exercise triggers the release of endorphins, natural stress-relievers that can help manage anxiety and restlessness often associated with ADHD. It provides a healthy outlet for excess energy and pent-up emotions.

Regulated Energy Levels: Regular exercise can help stabilize energy levels throughout the day, preventing the extreme highs and lows often experienced by individuals with ADHD. This can lead to better sustained attention and overall mood stability.

Establishing Routine: Structured exercise routines can provide a sense of predictability and routine, which can be especially beneficial for individuals with ADHD who thrive in consistent environments.

Sensory Integration: Certain types of exercise, like yoga or activities that involve balance and coordination, can improve sensory integration. This can help individuals with ADHD better process sensory information and reduce sensory overload.

Social Interaction: Participating in group exercise classes or team sports offers opportunities for social interaction, which can contribute to improved social skills and self-esteem in individuals with ADHD.

Better Sleep: Exercise can aid in regulating sleep patterns, helping individuals get more restful and restorative sleep. Improved sleep quality can in turn positively impact attention and mood.

Mind-Body Connection: Mindful exercises like yoga or tai chi promote mindfulness and self-awareness. These practices can help individuals with ADHD manage impulsivity and increase their ability to stay present.

It's important to note that while exercise can be beneficial, it's not a standalone treatment for ADHD. It should complement other strategies, such as medication and behavioral therapy, for comprehensive management. Before starting any exercise regimen, individuals with ADHD should consult their healthcare professionals to tailor a plan that suits their unique needs and abilities.

NUTRITION AND BRAINHEALTH
Nutrition plays a crucial role in brain health, affecting cognitive function, mood, and overall mental well-being. Consuming a balanced diet rich in essential nutrients can have a positive impact on brain health in various ways:

Omega-3 Fatty Acids: These healthy fats found in fish, flaxseeds, and walnuts are essential for brain development and function. Omega-3s support cognitive abilities, memory, and mood regulation.

Antioxidants: Foods high in antioxidants, such as berries, dark leafy greens, and colorful vegetables, help protect the brain from oxidative stress and inflammation, which can contribute to cognitive decline.

B Vitamins: B vitamins, particularly B6, B9 (folate), and B12, are important for maintaining healthy brain function. They play a role in producing neurotransmitters and preventing cognitive decline.

Protein: Amino acids from protein-rich foods support the production of neurotransmitters that regulate mood and cognitive function. Lean meats, fish, beans, and legumes are good sources of protein.

Complex Carbohydrates: Whole grains provide a steady supply of glucose to the brain, promoting sustained energy levels and mental alertness. They also help regulate mood by preventing drastic fluctuations in blood sugar.

Iron and Zinc: These minerals are vital for cognitive development, memory, and concentration. Foods like lean meats, beans, nuts, and whole grains are good sources of iron and zinc.

Vitamin D: Adequate vitamin D levels are linked to better cognitive function and mood regulation. Sources include fortified foods and sensible sun exposure.

Hydration: Staying hydrated is essential for optimal brain function. Even mild dehydration can affect mood, concentration, and cognitive performance.

Healthy Fats: Consuming sources of healthy fats like avocados, nuts, and olive oil supports brain cell structure and communication.

Limit Sugar and Processed Foods: Excessive sugar intake and highly processed foods can contribute to inflammation and negatively impact brain health over time.

Moderate Caffeine: While some caffeine intake can enhance alertness, excessive consumption may lead to anxiety and disrupted sleep, affecting overall brain health.

Mindful Eating: Practicing mindful eating can help regulate appetite and prevent overeating, promoting stable blood sugar levels and sustained mental focus.

It's important to remember that individual dietary needs may vary based on factors such as age, health conditions, and activity level. Consulting with a healthcare professional or registered dietitian can provide personalized guidance on nutrition for optimal brain health. Additionally, combining a balanced diet with other healthy lifestyle practices, such as regular exercise and sufficient sleep, further supports overall brain function and well-being.

UNLEASHING CREATIVITY AND PASSION

Unleashing creativity and passion involves nurturing your innate talents and interests. Here are some tips to help you tap into your creative side and fuel your passions:

Curiosity and Exploration: Stay curious about various subjects and activities. Explore new hobbies, read diverse materials, and engage with different art forms to expand your horizons.

Mindfulness and Presence: Practice mindfulness to be fully present in the moment. This can help you connect with your thoughts, feelings, and surroundings, leading to new insights and creative sparks.

Embrace Failure: Don't fear failure; see it as a stepping stone to growth. Many great ideas emerge from setbacks and mistakes.

Diverse Influences: Draw inspiration from a wide range of sources – literature, art, music, nature, and everyday life. Combining different influences can lead to unique and innovative ideas.

Create Regularly: Dedicate time to your creative endeavors regularly, even if it's just for a short period each day. Consistency nurtures creativity and helps you build momentum.

Surround Yourself: Connect with people who share your interests and passions.

Collaborative discussions can lead to fresh perspectives and breakthroughs.

Overcome Self-Doubt: Believe in your abilities. Self-doubt can hinder creativity. Replace negative self-talk with positive affirmations.

Seek Challenges: Step out of your comfort zone and take on challenges that ignite your passion. Pushing your boundaries can lead to incredible discoveries.

Capture Ideas: Keep a journal or digital notes to capture fleeting ideas. Inspiration can strike at any moment, and having a place to store your thoughts ensures you won't forget them.

Time for Play: Give yourself permission to play and experiment without strict goals. This playful mindset often leads to unexpected breakthroughs.

Limit Distractions: Find a space free from distractions where you can fully immerse yourself in your creative process.

Reflect And Refine: Regularly review and refine your work. Reflecting on your progress can help you identify areas for improvement and new directions.

Balance and Rest: Don't burn out. Balance your creative pursuits with self-care and rest to keep your passion alive.

Visualize Success: Imagine the end result of your creative projects. Visualizing success can motivate and inspire you to push forward.

Celebrate Achievements: Acknowledge your milestones and celebrate your achievements, no matter how small. Positive reinforcement fuels your passion.

Remember, creativity and passion are unique to each individual. Embrace your individuality, experiment with different techniques, and allow yourself the freedom to express your ideas in your own way.

CONCLUSION

In conclusion, navigating the realm of self-care for individuals with ADHD presents unique challenges and opportunities. Throughout this book, we've delved into the importance of tailored strategies that acknowledge the specific needs and preferences of those living with ADHD. From harnessing the power of routine and organization to embracing mindfulness techniques, the journey toward effective self-care requires a combination of patience, self-awareness, and a willingness to adapt.

It's evident that self-care isn't a one-size-fits-all concept. What works for one person might not work for another, and that's perfectly okay. The key lies in experimentation and a commitment to learning about oneself. Through trial and error, individuals with ADHD can discover their own toolkit of strategies that aid in managing their symptoms and promoting overall well-being.

As we conclude, remember that self-care isn't selfish—it's a necessary act of compassion toward oneself. It's about recognizing that taking care of your mental, emotional, and physical health equips you to navigate the world with greater resilience and clarity. By prioritizing self-care, individuals with ADHD can forge a path toward a more fulfilling and balanced life, one step at a time.

Printed in Great Britain
by Amazon

43306264R00046